Giacometti

and Frank Auerbach

Portraiture and the pursuit
of the absolute

Edward Lucie-Smith

Cv/Visual Arts Research Series 211

**Giacometti and Frank Auerbach
Portraiture and the pursuit
of the absolute**

Edward Lucie-Smith

Cv Publications www.tracksdirectory.ision.co.uk

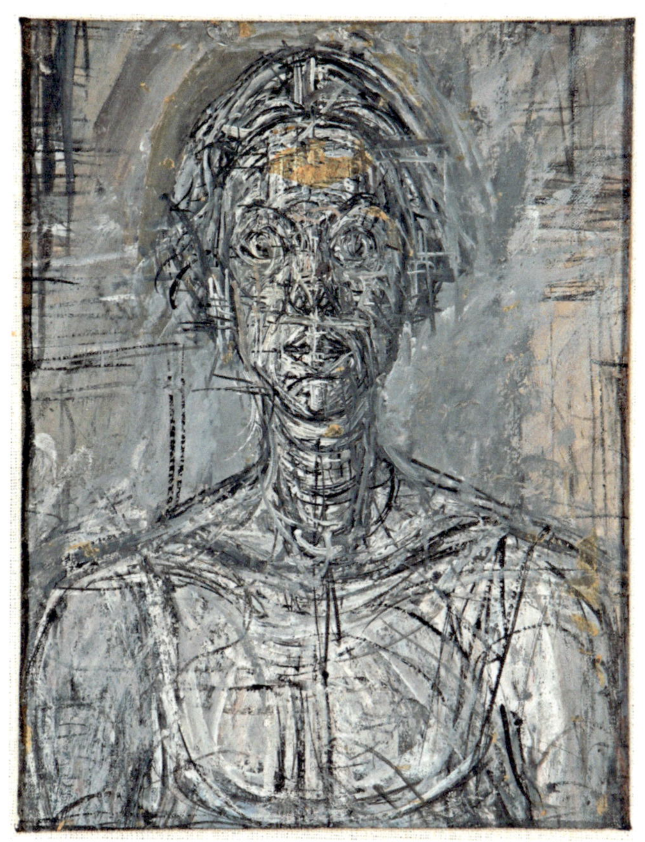

Bust of Annette by Alberto Giacometti, 1954
Private Collection © The Estate of Alberto Giacometti
(Fondation Giacometti, Paris and ADAGP, Paris) 2015

GIACOMETTI AND FRANK AUERBACH
Portraiture and the pursuit of the absolute

The coincidence of two exhibitions in major London institutions, one at the National Portrait Gallery, devoted wholly to Giacometti's work as a portraitist, the other a retrospective devoted to the career of Frank Auerbach, with a high proportion of portraits, on view at Tate Britain, prompts some reflections on the role of portraiture in contemporary art.

In theory, the role of the portraitist, as this existed before the rise of the Modern Movement, is kaput. There is no longer a place for it in the range of things that can usefully pre-occupy the ambitious painter or sculptor. The role of recording society, and in particular its most prominent members – their physical appearance, characteristic gestures and usual modes of dress – has been almost completely taken over by the professional photographer.

It is interesting, for example, to compare both these shows with another that is also on view in London a the same moment – the exhibition of portraits by Goya at the National Gallery. Goya presents the viewer with a whole cosmos.

Here is Europe, moving towards, into and then through the great social upheaval of the Napoleonic Wars, with particular emphasis on events within the Iberian Peninsula. Here are major political and social actors, as Goya encountered them. His portraits often convey acute moral and social judgments, but these are always subtly expressed. However sharp the characterisations (and they are sometimes given an astonishingly sharp edge, as for example in the full length likeness of Ferdinand VII - newly restored to his throne after the Napoleonic interregnum, and not at all improved by his experience of exile), they stick to the convention that the portraitist is a paid servant, forever secondary to the personality he is using his skills to immortalise.

This is absolutely not the case with the people portrayed by Giacometti and Auerbach. The balance of power has shifted. Now it is the artist who is dominant, and the subject of the portrait who submits. The sitter patiently submits himself or herself to the wishes and needs to the artist. The subjects do not have to be generally known — their position in the world outside of the studio is of no interest to the creator of the portrait. What is required is some kind of mysterious exchange, one might even describe it as a fusion of souls, memorialised by the artwork that results.

Of course portraits of this peculiarly intimate kind do have roots in some of the things that have happed in the art of the past – both before the Modern Movement began and in the earlier years of Modernism.

A prime early source for portraits of this kind is the long series of self-portraits by Rembrandt, and, in particular, the series that Rembrandt made in the closing years of his life. In each of these he seems to probe the essence of his own nature – to expose himself fully and truthfully to the spectator.

The 19th century Romantics were naturally interested in this aspect of self-portraiture – one sees more than traces of it in some of the role-playing self-portraits of Courbet. In Bonjour, M. Courbet, he seeks to establish himself as being at least the equal of his patron the industrialist Alfred Bruyas, who doffs his hat and takes off his glove in order to shake the artist's hand.

For a major sequence of self-portraits, ready to rival those of Rembrandt, we have to wait until the later years of the century, and the appearance of Vincent Van Gogh, who, more than any other artist of the period, defines himself through his sequence of self portraits.

A series of self-portraits of somewhat similar status was produced, from the 1990s to the 1940s, by the leading Norwegian artist, Edvard Munch. Two of the best-known come from the beginning and end of his career – the earlier being the lithograph *Self Portrait with Skeleton Arm*, which dates from 1895, and the latest being the painting Self Portrait Between Clock and Bed, which dates from 1940-44. Both show Munch as being obsessed with the idea of mortal fragility. "I was born dying," he claimed. "Sickness, insanity and death were the dark angels standing guard at my cradle and they have followed me throughout my life."

A contemporary of Munch's, the short-lived Austrian artist Egon Schiele (1890-1918), pushed things even further, not only through a series of startling self-portrait drawings, a number of which show the artist naked, but through his obsessional portrayals of a favourite model, Wally Neuzil, who met the artist in 1911, and who lived with him until they broke up abruptly in 1915. The relationship between the two was recently addressed in an exhibition held this year at the Leopold Museum in Vienna. It's clear that, for Schiele, Neuzil was a kind of 'other self' – an alternative identity. The contorted erotic poses in which he depicts Wally are often close to the equally contorted poses he adopts in his own self-portrait drawings. There is no doubt that we are meant to see them as being essentially twin souls.

Another artist who needs to be looked at in this connection is, of course, Picasso, who repeatedly featured his lovers in his work. Prominent in his later output are likenesses of his mistresses Marie-Thérèse Walter, Dora Maar, Françoise Gilot and – finally – Jacqueline Roque, whom Picasso met in 1953 and married in 1961. He painted more than 70 portraits of Jacqueline in the course of a single year – an obsessional pattern mirroring that to be seen in both the Giacometti and Auerbach exhibitions. In their cases, however, not all the sitters revisited so repeatedly are female, though a large number of them in fact are. One does not find this repetitive pattern in earlier artistic epochs. It is only the artist's own self-portrait that is sometimes often recreated, and then not until the 17th century, by Rembrandt in particular.

It is, I think, in order to look for possible reasons for this phenomenon, especially when it coincided so exactly with the time when the painted or sculptured portrait seemed to be losing its once primary position in Western art production, a loss of traction surely only partially due to the democratisation of portraiture by photography.

Making portraits first occupied this premium situation, as a leading form of artistic expression, in certain Ancient cultures – one thinks here of the numerous images of Egyptian pharaohs, many of which do indeed seem to strive for individual likeness, rather than offering generalised images of majesty. The standard portrait of the so-called 'heretic pharaoh', Akhenaten, with its elongated skull, offers a case in point. Ancient Roman statues and busts show intense interest in human physiognomy. This interest continued somewhat intermittently throughout what we now call the Middle Ages, and was revived very strongly with the European Renaissance. Essentially there were two factors here – the need for images of human beings who seemed to be in one way or another important to the societies they lived in, plus an ever-increasing fascination in the subtleties of human character. In particular, about the way these subtleties were expressed in outward human appearances.

The 17th century, the epoch of Rembrandt's search for the self through the medium of the visual arts, was also te period at which various major rationalist philosophical systems began to manifest themselves. That is to say, it the age of René Descartes (1596-1650), Blaise Pascal (1623-1662), Baruch Spinoza (1623-1677), John Locke (1632-1704) and Gottfried Wilhelm Leibniz (1646-1716).

In many ways, the reaction of both Giacometti and Frank Auerbach towards this evolution of thought, and the attitudes towards human personality and its interpretation that went with it, seems to be a contrarian one. Giacometti's art, in particular, is often aligned with the Existentialist philosophy that was so influential in the French intellectual circles of his time. Jean-

Paul Sartre wrote two influential essays about his work. The first, entitled The Quest for the Absolute, appeared in the catalogue for Giacometti's first solo exhibition in New York, held at the Pierre Matisse Gallery in 1948. The second, called simply The Paintings of Giacometti, was published in the catalogue for Giacometti's 1954 show at the Galerie Maeght in Paris.

Sartre saw Giacometti as an artist who, in terms of the human representations he made, was "starting again from zero" – that is, starting totally without preconceptions of any kind about what the human being he was regarding either looked like or should look like. Or, indeed, about the inner nature of the subject concerned. Giacometti, according to Sartre, was "always mediating between nothingness and being." His aim was "to give perceptible expression to pure presence." The title given to the current NPG exhibition follows the Existentialist party line exactly. It is called Giacometti: Pure Presence.

Much the same things can be said and, indeed, are very often said, about the portrait paintings made by Auerbach.

However, when I, perhaps rather crassly, start to put these two very similar artists into a broader context that certain doubts begin to manifest themselves. One notes the claustrophobic circumstances in which their art was made. The same routine, day after day. The same tiny circle of subjects. Not all of these subjects are completely undistinguished, speaking in purely worldly terms, but most of them are. In Giacometti's case many of them belong to his immediate family – his mother, his brother and studio assistant Diego, his wife Annette, his perhaps-mistress, who went by the name of 'Caroline' (which was not her own). A couple of collectors – David Thompson and David Sainsbury, one American, one British. The writer, Jean Gênet. James Lord, the American who was to be Giacometti's biographer. Others seem completely random: Nelda Negrini, a waitress who lived in Giacometti's native Stampa in Switzerland; Eli Lotar, a down-and-out jobbing photographer who was a friend of Caroline in the night-world of Montmartre. Somewhat incongruously, it is a figure of Lotar that presides over Giacometti's grave at Borgonovo, where the artist was born.

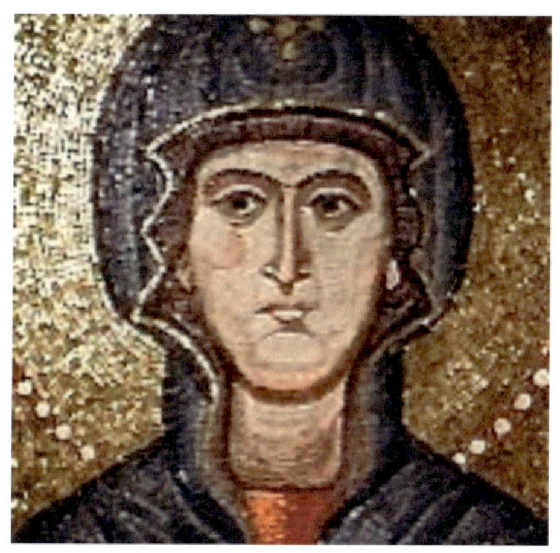

Madonna. Mosaico di arte costantinopolitana,
della fine dell'XI/inizio del XII secolo.
Esposto nel Museo civico medievale a Bologna.

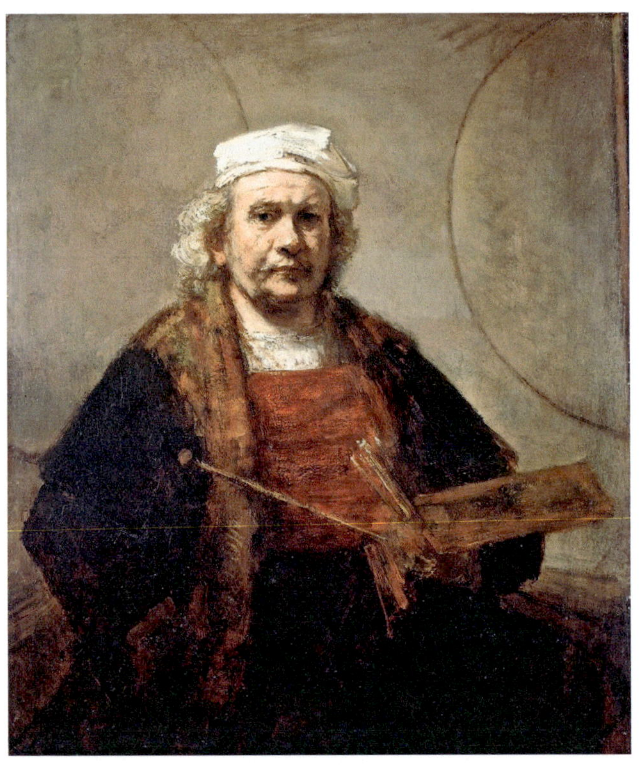

Rembrandt (1606-69)
Self Portrait with Two Circles about 1665-9
Kenwood House, The Iveagh Bequest,
English Heritage, London

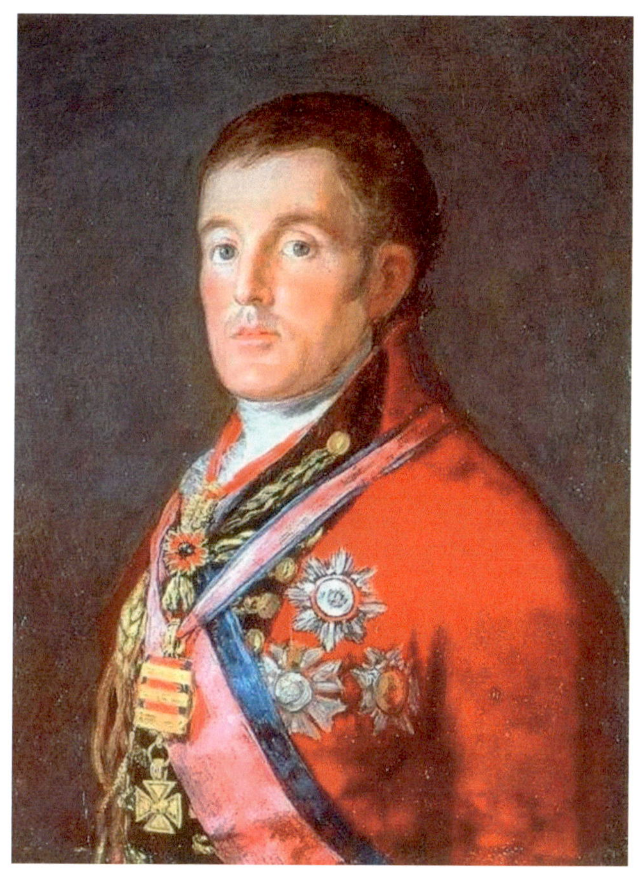

Francisco Goya (1746-1828)
Portrait of the Duke of Wellington
1812–14
Oil on canvas
National Gallery, London

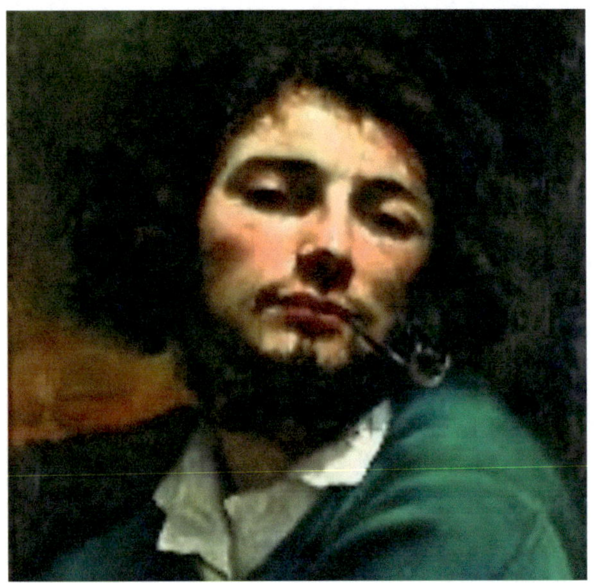

Gustave Courbet (1819–1877)
Gustave Courbet (1819-1877)
Self-portrait with Pipe
circa 1849
17 3/4 x 14 5/8 in. (45 x 37 cm)
Musée Fabre

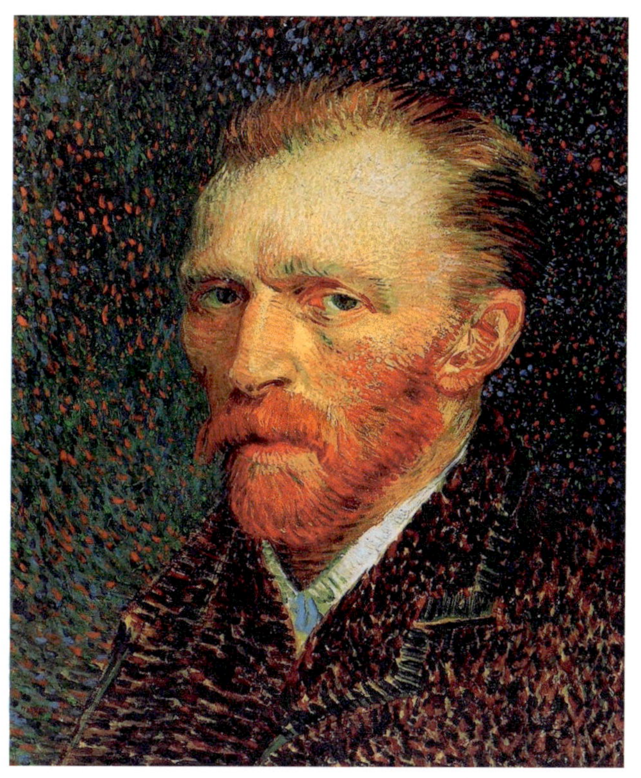

Vincent van Gogh 1863-1890
Self Portrait 1887
Oil on canvas
Art Institute of Chicago, Chicago, IL, USA

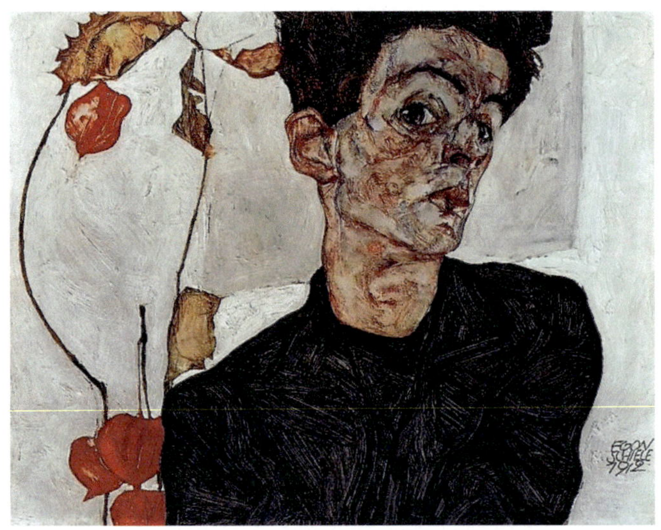

Egon Schiele (1890–1918)
German: *Selbstporträt mit Lampionfrüchten 1912*
oil and gouache on wood 32.2 × 39.8 cm (12.7 × 15.7 in)
Leopold Museum

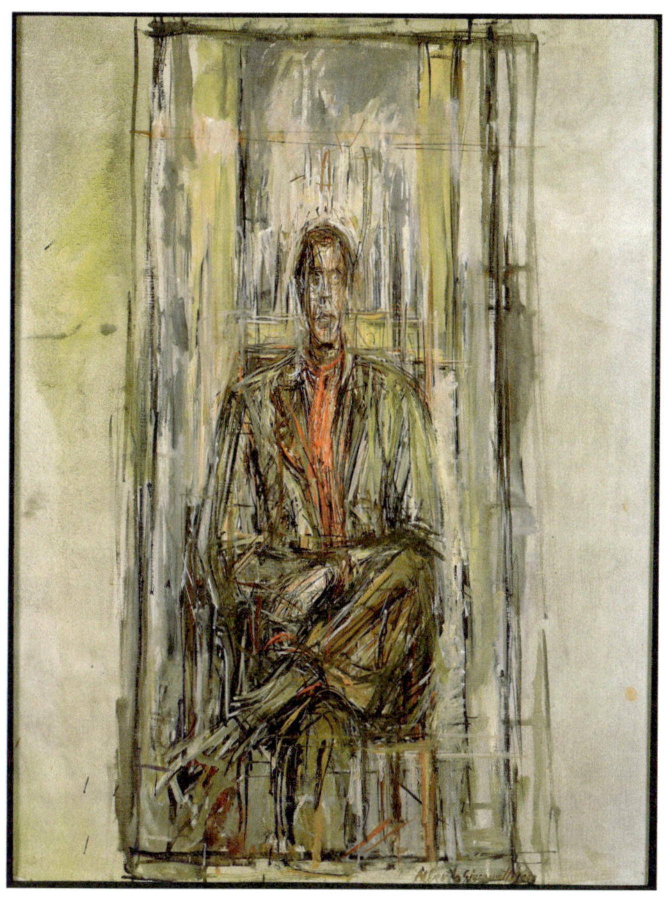

Diego Seated by Alberto Giacometti, 1948; Robert and Lisa Sainsbury Collection,
Sainsbury Centre for Visual Arts, University of East Anglia
© The Estate of Alberto Giacometti (Fondation Giacometti,
Paris and ADAGP, Paris) 2015; Photo: James Austin

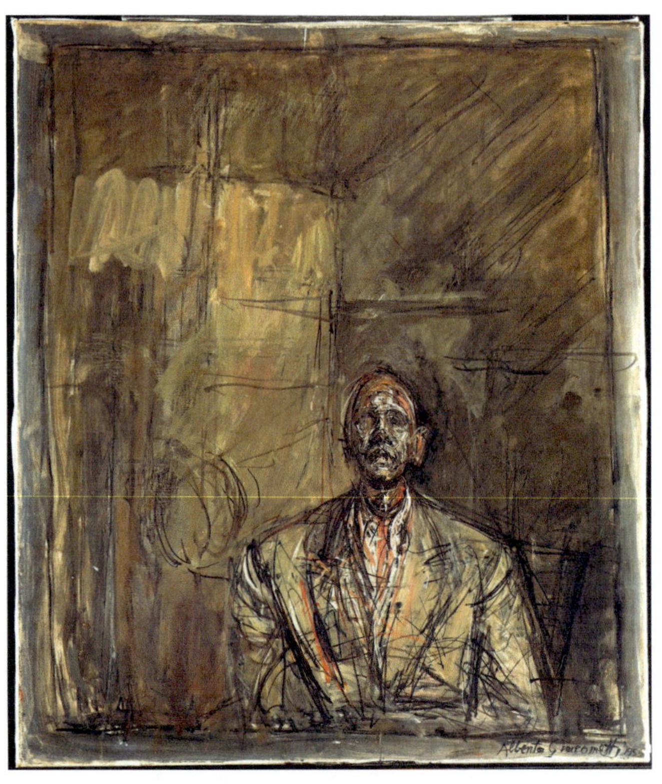

Jean Genet by Alberto Giacometti, c1954-5; Tate London 2015 © The Estate of
Alberto Giacometti (Fondation Giacometti, Paris and ADAGP, Paris) 2015

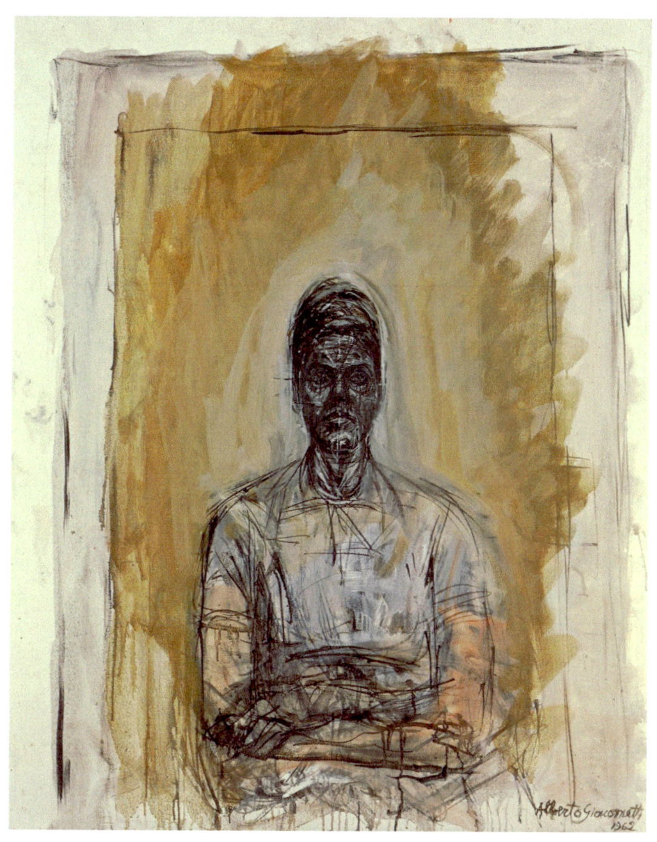

Caroline by Alberto Giacometti, 1961; Fondation Beyeler, Riehen / Basel, Beyeler
Collection © The Estate of Alberto Giacometti (Fondation Giacometti, Paris and
ADAGP, Paris) 2015; Photo: Robert Bayer, Basel

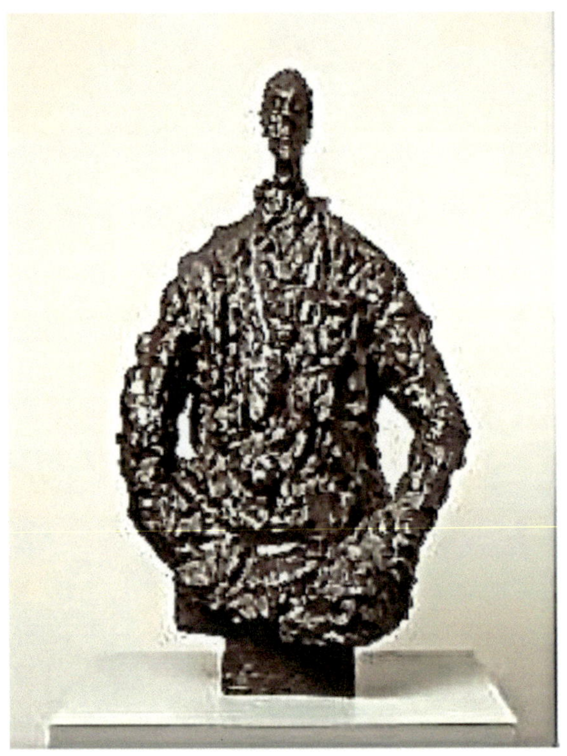

Diego in a sweater by Alberto Giacometti, 1953; Kunsthaus Zurich, Alberto
Giacometti-Stiftung © The Estate of Alberto Giacometti
(Fondation Giacometti, Paris and ADAGP, Paris) 2015

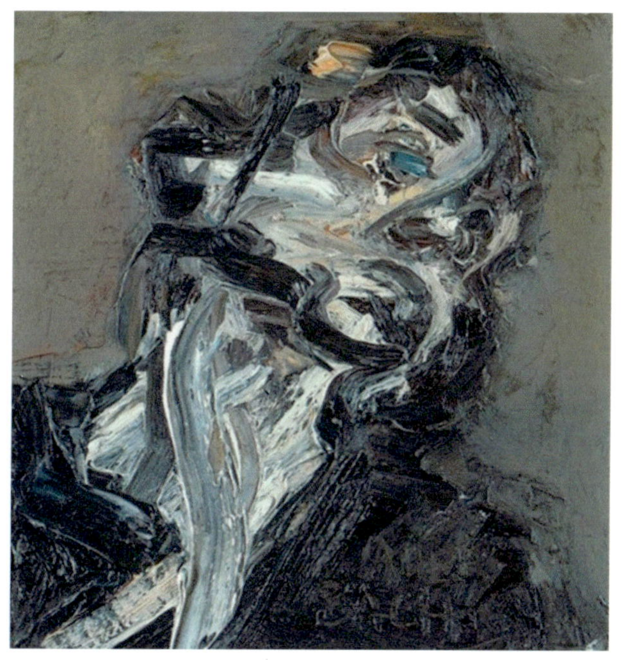

Frank Auerbach (b 1931)
Head of J.Y.M ll 1984-85
Oil on canvas 660 x 610 mm

Private collection © Frank Auerbach

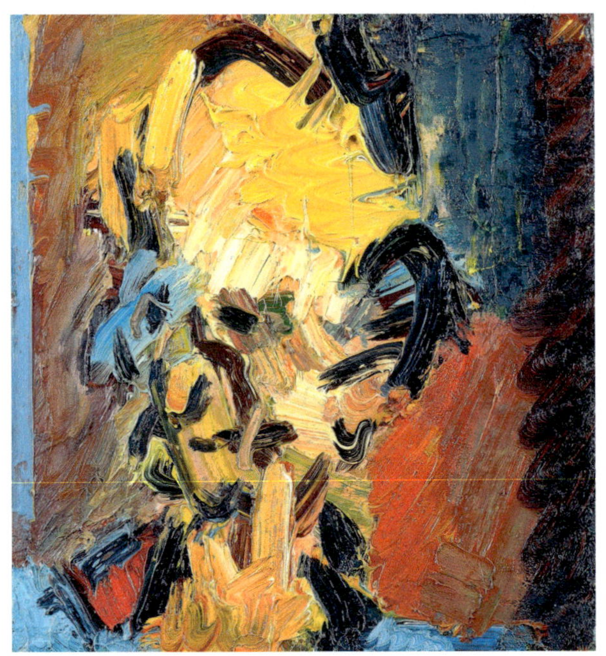

Frank Auerbach (b 1931)
Head of William Feaver 2003
Oil paint on board 451 x 406 mm
Collection of Gina and Stuart Peterson
© Frank Auerbach, courtesy Marlborough Fine Art

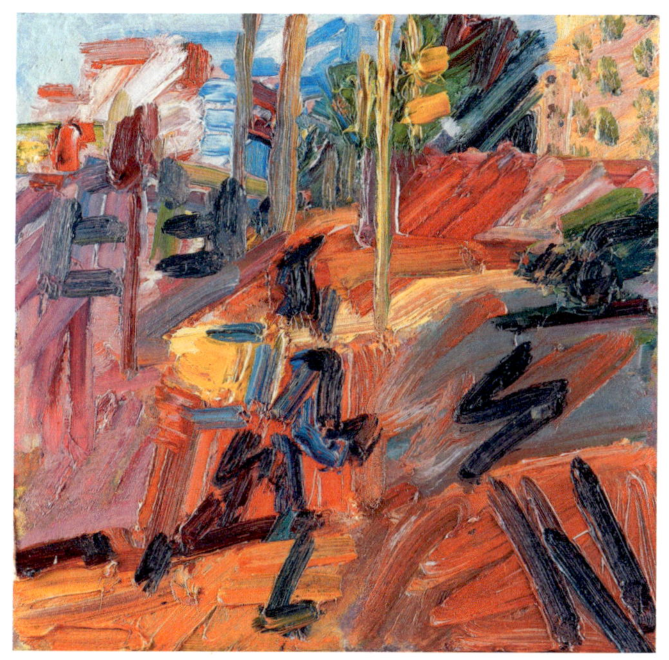

Frank Auerbach (b 1931)
Mornington Crescent 1965
Oil paint on board 1016 x 1270 mm
Private collection © Frank Auerbach,
courtesy Marlborough Fine Art

The narrative, here, is in some ways very much like the narrative surrounding the lives of other celebrated Modernist and Post Modernist artists – the ones who do not want to involve themselves in politics or in major social causes. Even Picasso, in old age, aimed to live a life of that kind, safely guarded from outsiders. Their wariness of the mass public is more than understandable, given the stresses imposed on successful artists in our age of celebrity culture. It is, however, impossible to claim that the strange, self-selected praetorian groups – relatives, lovers, friends, facilitators, sycophants and hangers-on - surrounding these creators contain many personalities who are of interest purely on their own merits, or for their own sake.

We look at Goya's portrait of the Duke of Wellington, now on view at the National Gallery, out of interest in the Duke, as well as out of interest in the artist who made it. We examine the series of Giacometti portraits at the NPG strictly out of interest in Giacometti's attitudes towards the mystery of human personality. The same is true of the portraits, some of subjects known only by their initials, included in the Auerbach retrospective at Tate Britain. It is the act of seeing, and the kind of seeing, that interests us, not, specifically, the person represented.

The idea – one might even say the myth – being put forward is that the artist, looking again and at certain people, who have become very familiar to him simply from their willingness to subject themselves over and over to his gaze, with each sitting "starting again from zero", just as Sartre suggests, will, through this laborious process, somehow penetrate to an otherwise inaccessible core of personality or 'being'. In other words, ordinary observation having failed, faith must take its place.

If one looks at Giacometti's portraits, and also at those made by Auerbach, seeking 'likeness', using that term in a purely conventional sense – the way in which we might use it regarding a particular sitter whom we already know in the flesh, or even whom we know through what seems to be a good photograph – we are immediately aware that the images these artists present to us do not satisfy these everyday, commonplace criteria.

The comparison that irresistibly comes to mind, for example, when looking at the portraits of Caroline – Giacometti made over 30 of these in his last phase, from 1960 to 1965, and six are in the NPG show – are with Byzantine art in its grandest phase, specifically with images of the Virgin gazing majestically out at us. Caroline, real name Poiraudeau, was educated in a reform school and had close links with the Parisian underworld of the 1950s and 1960s, though she always denied being a prostitute. Artist and sitter first met in 1958, but their friendship grew much closer in 1960, when Caroline was arrested for theft, and the artist worked to secure her release.

In Giacometti's portraits, and also in some characteristic ones by Auerbach, one seems to find the artist passionately searching for a spiritual dimension that no longer securely exists. There also seems to be a implied claim that by narrowing things down, this element can somehow be captured, even in the face of the multiple complexities and doubts imposed on both the artist and his subjects by contemporary society.

Giacometti's success with the public, and the equal respect and success enjoyed by Auerbach, now widely regarded as the senior surviving master of the contemporary British school, indicate that there is an undoubted appetite for what they both have to offer.

The wider context, however, is perhaps a little depressing. As I've suggested, in Rembrandt's late self-portraits we do see an exploration of the idea of what it is to be human, which can, in turn, by aligned with the variant forms of humanist philosophy that emerged in Europe during the course of the 17th century. From that, there is a progression, conspicuous in the work of leading artists of the late 19th and 20th centuries, to the idea of the artist recording himself as the central protagonist in a self-created myth, to which other leading actors are occasionally admitted. As for example, one sees in the paintings and drawings that Schiele devoted not only to himself but to his lover of the time, Wally Neuzil. Or, perhaps, in a less-focussed way, in the series of paintings that Picasso devoted, turn by turn, to a sequence of mistresses and then to his second wife, Jacqueline, whom he portrayed at least as often as Giacometti portrayed Caroline.

What none of these works – either by Schiele or Picasso – possesses, in contrast to those by Giacometti and Auerbach under consideration here, is something which makes the comparison with Byzantine art doubly relevant. To quote from the web-site of the Metropolitan Museum of Art: "In Byzantine theology, the contemplation of icons allowed the viewer direct communication with the sacred figure(s) represented." The Modernist or Post Modernist difference is that the icon painter actually contemplate a livinf person, not just the idea of a person, in order to re-create and transmit the sensation received.

In fact, these two shows can be thought of as making a contribution to the increasing tendency for contemporary art to take refuge in regions that previously belonged to religion. It's not all that far a step from Giacometti's obsessive contemplation of Caroline to the reversal of that situation: members of the public invited serially to contemplate the performance artist Marina Abramovic in her Museum of Modern Art event (2012) The Artist Is Present.

Edward Lucie-Smith, London, November 2015

Bio-data

Alberto Giacometti was born October 10, 1901, in Borgonovo, Switzerland, and grew up in the nearby town of Stampa. His father, Giovanni, was a Post-Impressionist painter. From 1919 to 1920, he studied painting at the Ecole des Beaux-Arts and sculpture and drawing at the Ecole des Arts et Métiers in Geneva. In 1920, he traveled to Italy, where he was impressed by the works of Alexander Archipenko and Paul Cézanne at the Venice Biennale. He was also deeply affected by African and Egyptian art and by the masterpieces of Giotto and Tintoretto. In 1922, Giacometti settled in Paris, making frequent visits to Stampa, and occasionally attended Antoine Bourdelle's sculpture classes.

In 1927, the artist moved into a studio with his brother, Diego, his lifelong companion and assistant, and exhibited his sculpture for the first time at the Salon des Tuileries, Paris. His first show in Switzerland, shared with his father, was held at the Galerie Aktuaryus, Zurich, in 1927. The following year, Giacometti met André Masson, and by 1930 he was a participant in the Surrealist circle until 1934. His first solo show took place in 1932 at the Galerie Pierre Colle, Paris. In 1934, his first American solo exhibition opened at the Julien Levy Gallery, New York. During the early 1940s, he became friends with Simone de Beauvoir, Pablo Picasso, and Jean-Paul Sartre. From 1942, Giacometti lived in Geneva, where he associated with the publisher Albert Skira.

He returned to Paris in 1946. In 1948, he was given a solo show at the Pierre Matisse Gallery, New York. The artist's friendship with Samuel Beckett began around 1951. In 1955, he was honored with retrospectives at the Arts

Council Gallery, London, and the Solomon R. Guggenheim Museum, New York. He received the Sculpture Prize at the 1961 Carnegie International in Pittsburgh and the Grand Prize for Sculpture at the 1962 Venice Biennale, where he was given his own exhibition area. In 1965, Giacometti exhibitions were organized by the Tate Gallery, London, the Museum of Modern Art, New York, the Louisiana Museum, Humlebaek, Denmark, and the Stedelijk Museum, Amsterdam. That same year, he was awarded the Grand Prix National des Arts by the French government. Giacometti died January 11, 1966, in Chur.
Source: Guggenheim online

Frank Helmut Auerbach is a German-born British painter. He has been a naturalised British citizen since 1947. Auerbach was born in Berlin, the son of Max Auerbach, a patent lawyer, and Charlotte Nora Burchardt, who had trained as an artist. Under the influence of the British writer Iris Origo, his parents sent him to Britain in 1939 und...

Born: 29 Apr 1931 (age 84) · Berlin, Germany
Education: London South Bank University ·
Central Saint Martins · Royal College of Art
Children: Jake Auerbach (Son)
Periods: Modern art
1939: Aged seven, Auerbach left Germany via Hamburg on 4 April 1939 and arrived at Southampton on 7 April.
1942: Left behind in Germany, Auerbach's parents later died in a concentration camp in 1942.
1955: From 1955, he began teaching in secondary schools, but quickly moved into the visiting tutor circuit at numerous art schools, including Ravensbourne, Ealing, Sidcup and the Slade School of Art.

1994: Showing at the National Gallery in London in 1994 he made direct reference to the gallery's collection of paintings by Rembrandt, Titian and Rubens.

2001: In 2001, Auerbach was the subject of a television film entitled Frank Auerbach: To the Studio, directed by Hannah Rothschild and produced by Jake Auerbach (Jake Auerbach Films Ltd).

Source: Wikipedia

The Author Edward Lucie-Smith is an art critic and art historian, also a poet and photographer. He is generally regarded as the most prolific and widely published writer on contemporary art. Some of his books are used as standard texts throughout the world.

LONDON TERMINAL

FRIEZE ART FAIR 2013

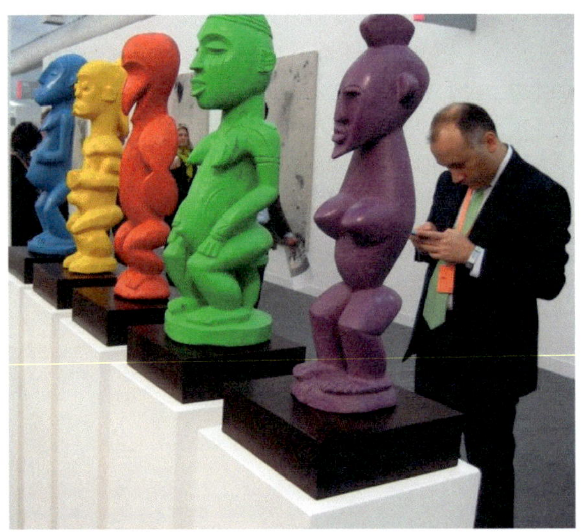

EDWARD LUCIE-SMITH

Cv/Visual Art Research Series 187

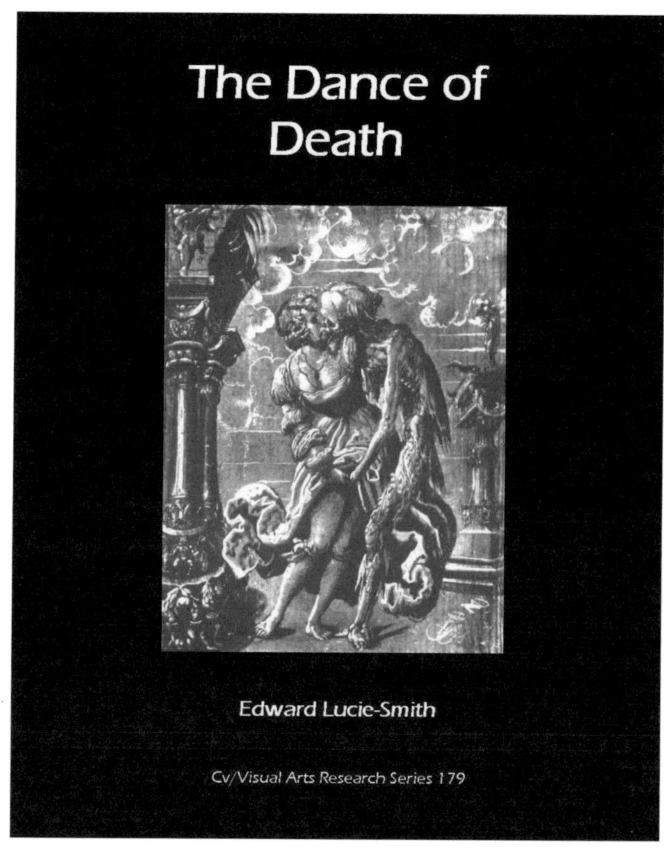

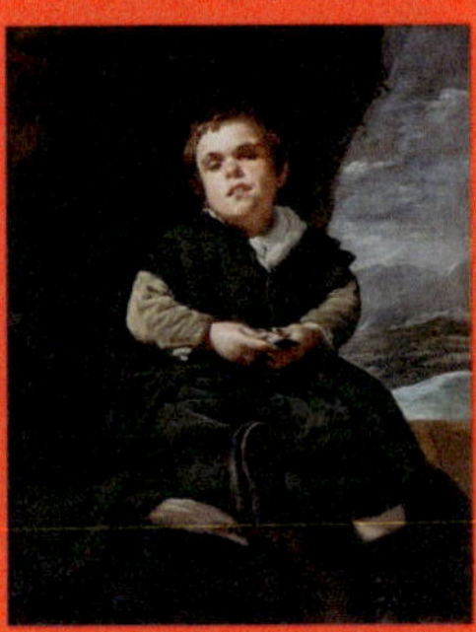

Edward Lucie-Smith
Uncollected Writings
Studies of Western Art
Cv/Visual Arts Research Series 152

Cv/Visual Arts Research Archive

THE DECLINE AND FALL
OF THE
AVANT-GARDE

ESSAYS ON CONTEMPORARY ART
BY EDWARD LUCIE-SMITH

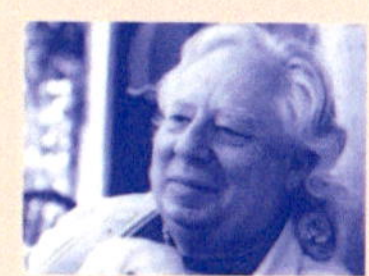

Cv/Visual Arts Research Series 161-175

Art . Travel . Histories .
Social Studies . Studio Work
Published by
Cv Publications
tracksdirectory.ision.co.uk

Made in the USA
Monee, IL
07 July 2026

56548184R00024